thief

in

the

interior

THIEF IN THE INTERIOR

Phillip B. Williams

ALICE JAMES BOOKS

FARMINGTON, MAINE

10 9 8 7 6 5 4 3 2 1

Alice James Books are published by Alice James Poetry Cooperative, Inc.,
an affiliate of the University of Maine at Farmington.

Alice James Books
114 Prescott Street
Farmington, ME 04938
www.alicejamesbooks.org

Library of Congress Cataloging-in-Publication Data

Williams, Phillip B.
  [Poems. Selections]
  Thief in the interior / Phillip B. Williams.
      pages cm
  Includes bibliographical references.
  ISBN 978-1-938584-17-6 (alk. paper)
  I. Title.
  PS3623.I5593A6 2016
  811'.6--dc23
                        2015005094

Alice James Books gratefully acknowledges support from individual donors, private foundations,
the University of Maine at Farmington, and the National Endowment for the Arts.

ART WORKS.
arts.gov

Cover Art: "Talib Kweli" by James Jean

contents

acknowledgments

Thank you to the editors who had faith in these poems and published them, sometimes in different versions, in the following journals:

Blackbird—"Prayer"
Callaloo—"Ignis Fatuus," "Misericorde"
Columbia Poetry Review—"Witness (When Rashsawn Brazell went missing…)" as "Cocoon"
Connotation Press: An Online Artifact—"For Joy Be Righteous"
Crab Orchard Review—"Of Shadows and Mirrors"
Forklift, Ohio—"Often I am Permitted to Return to the City"
Indiana Review—"Inheritance: The Force of Aperture" as an excerpt from "American Aesthetic: An Exhibition," "God as Failed Figuration," and "A Survey of Masculinity" as "History of Masculinity"
The Kenyon Review – "Luminous, Whatever Honey"
Kenyon Review Online—"Birth of the Doppelgänger"
Kinfolks Quarterly—"Inheritance: Anthem" as "
The Lifted Brow – "Witness (I called his name but…)", "Witness (Dear Ms. Brazell-Jones, In an interview…)", "Witness (as though to repair…)", and "Witness (Dear Ms. Brazell-Jones, I miss my brother…)"
Linebreak—"Greatly be Gentle"
Matter—"Witness (A friend tells me…)"
Nashville Review—"Black Witch Moth"
Obsidian – "Eleggua and Eshu Ain't the Same"
Oxford American – "Of Contour, Of Cadence"
Poetry—"Do-rag," "First Words" as "Speak," "Of Darker Ceremonies," "Vision in Which the Final Blackbird Disappears"
pluck!—"Inheritance: Spinning Noose Clears its Throat" as "Spinning Noose Clears its Throat"
The Paris-American—"Visitation"
The Rumpus—"Sonnet with a Cut Wrist and Flies"
Southern Indiana Review—"Selvage"

Toe Good – "Door to a War I Never Knew"
Tupelo Quarterly — "A Spray of Feathers, Black," "Apotheosis," "Epithalamium," and "Then as Proof the Land"

"Do-rag" appears in the anthology *Best New Poets 2014,* selected by Dorianne Laux

"Prayer" appears in the anthology *Please Excuse This Poem: 100 New Poets for the Next Generation*, edited by Brett Fletcher Lauer and Lynn Melnick

"Black Witch Moth", "Do-rag", "Misericord", and "Then as Proof the Land" appear in *Poets on Growth*, edited by Peter LaBerge and Talin Tahajian

For their encouragement, endless insight, and support during the creation of this book and its dozen drafts I thank: Catherine Barnett, Reginald Dwayne Betts, Remica Bingham, Jericho Brown, DéLana Dameron, Nicole Terez Dutton, Tarfia Faizullah, Aricka Foreman, Rachel Eliza Griffiths, James Allen Hall, Niki Herd, Richie Hofmann, Randall Horton, Ashaki Jackson, Monica Jimenez, Amanda Johnston, Bettina Judd, Corey Van Landingham, Rickey Laurentiis, Khadijah Queen, Treasure Shields Redmond, Justin Phillip Reed, Roger Reeves, Patricia Smith, KMA Sullivan, Marcus Wicker, Keith Wilson, and L. Lamar Wilson.

Thank you to Kathryn Davis, Kathleen Finneran, Cecily Stewart Hawksworth, and my peers at Washington University at St. Louis MFA for making my experience unforgettable.

Thanks for the generous gifts of time, financial support, and camaraderie to Toi Derricotte, Cornelius Eady, and Alison Meyers at Cave Canem; Michael Collier and Jen Grotz at the Bread Loaf Writers Conference; Dr. Charles Henry Rowell at the Callaloo Conference; Ron Mitchell and Marcus Wicker at the New Harmony Writers Conference; Natasha Trethewey and Kevin Young at Emory University; Rafia Zafar and Amy Gassel for the Chancellor Fellowship at Washington University in St. Louis; and Don Share and Christina Pugh for the Ruth Lilly Poetry Fellowship from The Poetry Foundation.

Special thanks to Janice Harrington, Tyehimba Jess, and Laura Kortiz for starting it all.

To Mary Jo Bang and Carl Phillips, thank you for teaching me with kindness, patience, and faith.

Endless thanks to Carey Salerno, Alyssa Neptune, and the Alice James Books cooperative board for believing in this collection. I can't imagine my first book being in better hands.

I finally want to thank my family for always encouraging me to do whatever I wanted to do in this one life I have. Thank you for allowing me to live in a way that brings me joy and hopefully makes you proud.

This book is dedicated to my father, Calvin Ford. R.I.P. I miss you.

I

BOUND

Wasn't night what lingered where sweat left
salt, where breath touch-expired? No.
I didn't find stars or the moon in my hair,
or grass, or the first traces of dew that I am told
cannot compete with a woman pleasured,
that I could get her that way and should try to,
should want to try—

                  Was a vastness over me
like a great system of clouds pursuing each other,
colliding into one another like fists that bloomed
like devotions like—

                  Can I be only one thing
at once? I was told to believe in and became that
single vessel beneath which water I would never taste
moved. I was shut tight. I was going somewhere
and quickly.

Little boat.

       Little boat made smaller by distance.

Black Witch Moth

The moth lifts its dress and everything beneath
its hem's shadow sings—the grasses where lie
the dead bull and flies skating across its still-
open eyes, its mouth crusted over with clover
and spit while the maggots swim their
patient circuits where the bull's genitals
have rotted and dropped their bells. The moth
slips through gnat-swarmed air onto the bull's hooves
and flies past the bull's corpse, beyond the outskirts
of the barnyard. No dust from the moth's pleats—
opening and closing—drops onto the dead
animal's choir. A boy sees its black dress bob
above him, sees in its shadow an angel to call his own.
Let a sudden finish overcome him wherever
the wild shadow lies flat its news, lies motionless
its wingdom among the barnyard grass.
Let the earth take in the boy as it will the bull.
And the worm-work done unto him as unto the bull.
His color gone and bone given into an end
making permanent the final pose of his suffering,
crux into crux his body returning into itself
as though into the first cell that split
until skin, until marrow, until muscle, until the maggot
is king over body. Let the boy's skin be a tearing,
to see it torn from him and wonder how
then wonder how far until the next time, the next boy.
The moth flashes open its dress then not,

flash then not, flaps over the dead boy, its shadow
moving up his thigh to the hip, to the torso,
lifting its garment across his nakedness.
And the bull into the earth. And the boy into the earth.
And the earth not full, the earth not full.

Ignis Fatuus

He is one of many points of light
              that seem, at first, distant enough
      to lead me away from my loneliness and toward
the flourish-stillness-flourish of the heart
              when told, *Imitate the varied stars that
      have failed to guide us; now imitate everything
beneath the stars.*

                              ~

But who is he? Phantom, filament at its brightest

before blowing out, pattern made pattern

because it was broken like a heart
              can never be, but say it anyway?

None of those. Deceit had a simpler face: violet

all around, every hemisphere familiar until turned.

                              ~

The stars and what lied beneath them have fled, spectral. What little light
poked through the branches has led you here. Lie down. I've tried to be kind
to you by keeping the sharpest instrument to myself.

First Words

A storm and so a gift.
        Its swift approach
                lifts gravel from the road.
A fence is flattened in
        the course of the storm's
                worse attempt at language —
thunder's umbrage. A tree
        is torn apart,
                blown upward through a bedroom
window. A boy winnows
        through the pile
                of shards for the sharpest parts
from the blown-apart
        glass. He has
                a bag that holds found edges
jagged as a stag's
        horns or smooth as
                a single pane smashed into
smaller panes that he sticks
        his hand inside
                to make blood web across
his acheless skin flexing
        like fish gills
                O-lipped for a scream
they cannot make.
        He wants to feel
                what his friends have felt,
the slant of fear on their faces

he could never
        recreate, his body born
without pain. When his skin's
     pouting welts
          don't rake a whimper
from his mouth, he runs
     outside, arms up
          for the storm, aluminum
baseball bat held out
     to the sky
          until lightning, with an electric
tongue, makes his viscera
     luminescent;
          the boy's first word for pain
     is the light's
          new word for home.

THEN AS PROOF THE LAND

Because when I write "tree" I mean fire
of autumn. I mean wind moves through the failing
leaves like a man the hue of bark, chased

into that height, into god-hood,
which is a silence. Every cypress
stakes its claim in
what could be called idyll, making a fetish
of the land.

I am the question. Branches answer,
It would be our pleasure, then, as proof, nod closer.

Inheritance: Spinning Noose Clears Its Throat

It
Is
Time
To
End
Child
Come
Let
Us
::::
Begin
With
Me
Effigy
Tragedy
Hollowed
Moon
Knowing
Where
To
Shine

To
Where
Know
I
But
Door
B ack
Out
Backed
Blacks

Laws
Black
Tongues
Black
Up
Coughing
Nation
One
Pallid
Nest
Come
O
Jim Crow
Old
As
Gabriel
Contortion
Elegant
Same
Dust
Is

Here I am the mainstay
Every fulcrum lifts and bows toward.
As far as I'm concerned, freedom
Desires no promise. Simply feet, strange horizons

Slave
Tarika Wilson
Rekia Boyd
Aiyana Stanley-Jones
the President

Is
Defined
By
Choking
Rocking
Back
And
Forth
Hated
Body
Remembers
Rope
Creak
No
Matter
If
For

Vision in Which the Final Blackbird Disappears

A monstrosity in the alley.
A many-bodied movement grouped
for terror, their flights' brief shadows
on the kitchen curtains, on the street's
reliquaries of loose squares and hustle.
Some minds are groomed for defiance. The youngest
calls out his territory with muscular vowels
where street light spills peculiar, his hand
a chorus of heat and recoil. Could have been
a doctor, say those who knew and did not
know him, though he never wanted to know
what gargles endlessly in a body—wet hives,
planets unspooled from their throbbing shapes.
There are many ways to look at this.
He got what he wished against. He got
wings on his shoes for a sacrifice. The postulate
that stars turn a blind eye to the cobalt corners
of rooms is incorrect. Light only helps or ruins sight.
Daylight does cruel things to a boy's face.

INHERITANCE: The Force of Aperture

"Accused Killers Had 3-Way Sex On Black Corpses?"—
BlackAmericaWeb.com (2-18-13) "Three Negroes lynched at
Duluth, Minn. for rape. Oct, 1919 by mps"—etching on photo
postcard of the lynching

Fascinated, spooked into desire, the jarring
appetites of the living. Some men soak
black skin in fiction and knock stories back
like a shotgunned body. Impartial, the ground,
trees, and rivers hold artifacts of flesh impaired
by those demanding privilege, their wild aesthetics.

~

Black bodies and their high aesthetic
value: teeth, toes, and severed penises in jars
strangely priced. A post card, violent mail,
shows the photo of three men lynched in Minnesota.
To look is to be welcomed by the white foreground
of faces like flashes lighting the spectacle, turning back.

~

Study these bodies, these leather-bound books back
to back, like a good pupil, I hear, then attempt art.
I read about two black boys strangled, made background
for moaning white bodies. Canopic jars
made of the mind, fetish museum made miniscule
by killers speculating darkly what the dead can bare.
Body a book of vulgarities: famine, ravage, jarring

11

light, encounter, theft. Savage not made new but grounded
in what was always possible. Flesh a morbid center
unwound, skin carved into familiars. Western artists
negrotized their brushes, painted African masks over bare
canvas. Did aesthetes go blind when the myth looked back?

~

Were Misters Clayton, McGhie, and Jackson beautiful
portraits hung in Duluth, Minnesota?
Were Misters Glover and Rankins rare collections? The snare
of white faces stark against night's mocking background
caught me looking in, caught me imagining backs
bent as though before kings, our mouths open like jars—

~

Our dead, once forced to reject the ground
for rope and air—sky hued erotic there
in the leaves—now forced to the ground, backed
into morning headlines, their minced codas
between weather and traffic, a jarring revision:
white writhing over black, the American aesthetic.

God as a Failed Figuration

A reflection, a figment of a figment
of the imagination. The male figure stands
by himself, obscured. When he lifts his hands
lightning scythes below. From his weary blues
blues spill out but nothing around can
define how. Emptily the blues signify.

INHERITANCE: ANTHEM

or made to fall so flail made fallen angel or made to fall so flail angel made fallen as he is alone in the street scored his that history bore into moments and clavicle sternum and ant mandible clamped for and skull curve ground to sunlight and not much more and the door to hunger to a mirror forced to mirror a mirror more toward toward's never-born semaphore future fastens tightly to tall-tale tallies of the past passing everlastingly so the corridor poured poorly toward that what was before is now our hour every hour and on before shuts to open once feeding for nature knows hunger into dust gored by hours of omens pestle-and-mortared with entrance and exit wounds him to fell him and failure is Subdued angel made un-ang-el figure is

impact...or, myth does not radiate from the target, rather the target calls myth to its core.

The choreography is simple. Be followed. Be pulled over. Smile. He doesn't smile back when he returns your license. Step out of the car. "Is something wrong?" Get out of the car. He tells you you smell funny. You say "nag champa," say "shea butter." You don't smoke. Flashlight through your back window. What you doing with all those race books? You're all-but-dissertation. He has a gun. You are sure you teach his daughter about sit-ins and assassinations. When backup comes they both lecture you for thirty minutes. You were on your way to a funeral. You will miss the open casket to avoid your own.

"How did he—?" "How long the stench?" "How many did it take to—?" [Smoke leaks from forced-open flesh doors] "Were you of authority?" "Who authorized?" "What color was—?" "Did he know his name—?" [Wilting goes as quickly as memory allows] "Was he shot before or after—?" "How many entered from—?" "Who saw who see whom?" [E-v-i-d-e-n-c-e spells *hand over mouth*] "But, Sir, the form requests that we follow—" "The procedure has been—" "Who arranged him like this?" "Where did he throw the weapo—?" "There was no—?" "How long did it take for—?" "Were you afraid?" [Ceremonies solidify the contract that makes exotic the rot of other] "Were there flies?" "Was there the smell of grease?" "Did they sing?" "The people, when they came outside, did they sing?" [To must be flawless to be made martyr]

I woke up like dis! I woke up like dis!

In a city closer than you think, the antagonist is anchored to his uncivility. His tribe defies, by nature, nature, carries the illness of loud music and theft bagged in felonious rancor. Savage borne thus innocuous, by constitution, to citizens. Assumed diseased: Ebola, drapetomania, man-made cruelties pandemical, but don't say. Say science. Say vaccine with a slow tongue: Tu-ske-gee. Phenotypical response to metal bit and bloodsalt swelling. Making dog sounds. Clichéd Animalia. Only one man can save the world from these fiends before they scratch the earth like black roosters to voodoo. O nomenclature, O clenched omens.

Please turn off all cellular devices!

Riiiiiiiiing!!!!!

Recording of this incident is prohibited!

These events have been copyrighted for future use!

Viewer discretion is advised!

Riiiiiiiiing!!!!!

Riiiiiiiiing!!!!!

Shhhh! You gone miss the good part!

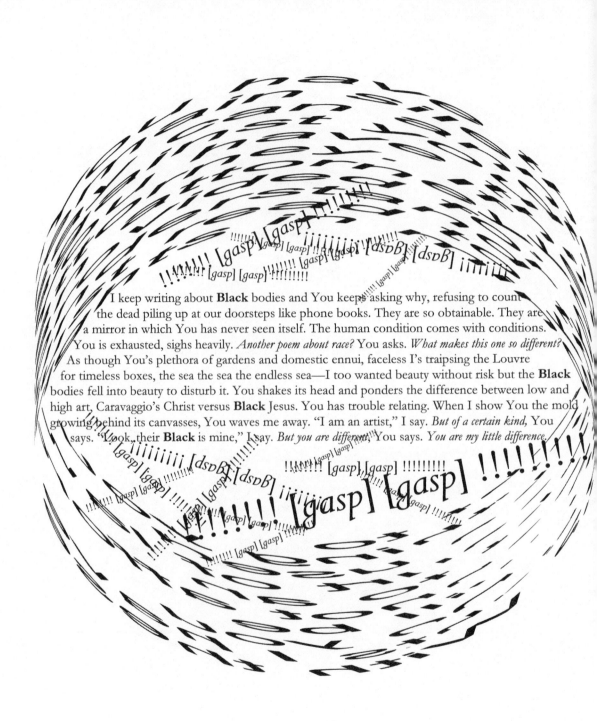

I keep writing about **Black** bodies and You keeps asking why, refusing to count
the dead piling up at our doorsteps like phone books. They are so obtainable. They are
a mirror in which You has never seen itself. The human condition comes with conditions.
You is exhausted, sighs heavily. *Another poem about race?* You asks. *What makes this one so different?*
As though You's plethora of gardens and domestic ennui, faceless I's traipsing the Louvre
for timeless boxes, the sea the sea the endless sea—I too wanted beauty without risk but the **Black**
bodies fell into beauty to disturb it. You shakes its head and ponders the difference between low and
high art, Caravaggio's Christ versus **Black** Jesus. You has trouble relating. When I show You the mold
growing behind its canvasses, You waves me away. "I am an artist," I say. *But of a certain kind,* You
says. "Look, their **Black** is mine," I say. *But you are different,* You says. *You are my little difference.*

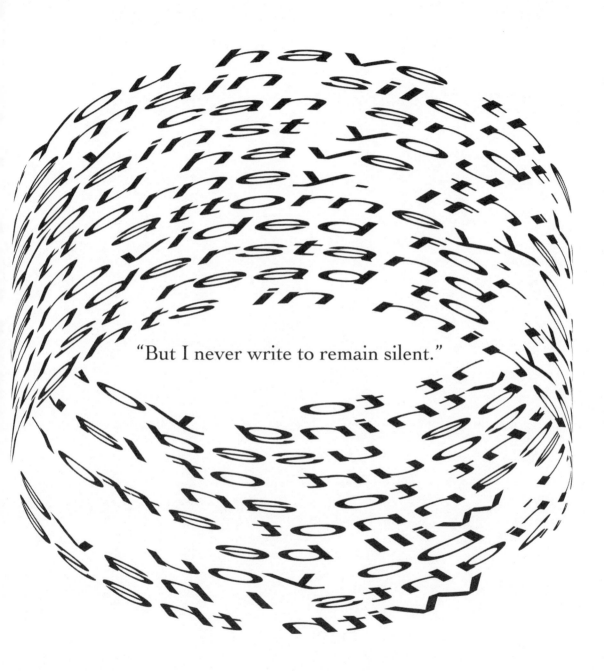

"But I never write to remain silent."

SONNET WITH A CUT WRIST AND FLIES

I.

blade to the soft and the soft flashed open
 was the breakage of robins

II.

blood dripped to the floor
 splashed on the tile   painted a big toe

III.

the slit would talk back   sweet nothing in a red gown

IV.

*wrist [rist] **noun** 1. the carpus or lower part
 of the forearm where it joins the hand.*

to explore the joint   window
 hinged on the edge
 of the body

 to slice it   to peek into the cut
and find the ribbon

V.

blood veined by the rhapsodic

VI.

a single mouth its total face

VII.

risk [risk] **verb** *2. to expose to the chance of injury*
or loss; hazard: to risk one's life

as the mind was made enterable   a boy stepped into
        was natural in him   was his
    and spectacular

VIII.

an artery's plucked quatrains
    perfected through wreckage   a man
        waited in the pulse

IX.

a man found in the wrist who wanted out but who
      put him in?

X.

he spoke the four languages of the heart
    he would   touch   the boy   would

XI.

hurt the boy and translate his screams
    into a fifth vernacular

XII.

the boy he entered   was put into   no more
    than an urn   than a tawdry vessel

XIII.

sacrifice [sák-re-fīse] **noun** *1. a giving up of something valued*
for someone or something else considered to be of more value

the radius giving itself to the ulna
      the man   himself hidden in the dark creases
of vein-rope and contraction
        an artery's hierophant drum
the man

XIII.

stepped out of the dark and into where the cut
     welcomed the room's wattage

XIII.

stepped into the light his face a cut
     a black hyphen from which all speech

XIII.

from which all darkness was made legible

XIII.

the single mouth his total face

XIII.

he would touch and call himself many names

XIII.

call himself a god but he was no god

XIII.

but was easy to believe him a god
     to walk to him to relive how he got there

XIII.

stutter and suck

XIII.

was the sound of the cut closing
        in on them both to hold them there

XIII.

as before in the dark when no one was around
        blood wild with knowledge

XIII.

the man approached   was a knowledge himself
        his face the one written page

XIII.

his option the sole option
            he would take the boy
    be mnemonic
        be what had always been prefaced to

        he reached out his hand

XIV.

and his fingers—thumbnail carving
        the boy's cheek—touched   like flies

A Spray of Feathers, Black

Angels know me by scent alone. Precise
is their reaping my confessions. I am stained.
God is stainless. A crescent moon pierces

the night. Stars: wounds grouped and sainted
as constellations. I counted my blows, dared
the bruises to implode like dying suns. Instead,

they hid behind skin to mask their dread.
Blood, my citizens, I speak as a creed-lit
failure, faith in me a venom, adder-

fire if the adder were God. I cried, *Let
me feel You like Abraham poised to sever
Isaac, though I am filth, am derelict.*

Look how a lilt of dust is built to serve,
sits on the lips like a song with no verse.

PRAYER

Help me distinguish between approaching blizzard
and his breath against my ear, causing my skin
to whistle like a blade of grass. Please, help me keep
my mind at ease when he trembles beneath me, cold-
hot and wet, wet all over. The sheets have been
soaked and wrung and bleached. The carpet
vacuumed, the kitchen floor swept. God, help me keep
a clean home, keep the roaches' running prayers
from competing with my own, keep the rats
from gnawing on the bread with filth and squeak.
Plastic won't keep ice crystals from making
a second pane over the window, won't keep
the don't-give-a-damn cold from coming in
and lingering beneath our feet. Give me feet
that can sing, that can sing all over this floor
like a drum battalion, stomp out the pests
and their late night coitus, stomp out winter
crawling from beneath the floorboard, stomp out
the fever pouring from his never-dry back.
I want to heal like You do. God, let me walk on water.

MISERICORDE

Silence: the body down, as expected.

A sweet burn nets the room:
incense, nightcap, decay's sudden lift. A bee

circles your open mouth, lands on your open eye's near-dry curve.

Dizzy, it gathers its reflection
in your irises' dull glass
and shivers pollen onto your still eyelash.
Is this what is meant by

enter the light?: golden fur, golden dust, golden stain;

how I'd wrap you
around my shoulder,
a final possession — camouflage;
cataract, silk.

O to wear you: a gown

over which bees weave the scent of wet grass, wet
as though expecting —

You are powerless.

I shut your eyes with my hand, your mouth
with my mouth.

II

WITNESS

According to America's Most Wanted, *"Around 3:00 a.m.
on February 17, 2005, New York City transit workers found
two suspicious bags alongside the track at the Nostrand Avenue
station in Brooklyn."*

When Rashawn Brazell went missing,
the first trash bag of his body parts
hadn't seen his head, didn't know where
it could be. The subway tracks spat
no sparks for him; the stairway light
to the train flickered no S.O.S.;
the recycling plant uncoiled
no ribbon of six-pack plastic to offer
evidence, condolence. Workers
at the recycling plant found a morbid gift,
limbs bagged up like trash. No head
to say a name or claim his body scattered
like false clues across Brooklyn. A shovel
holds memory better than any mourner,
rain carrying the sweet sting of pine
in its translucent purse, bird shit
from a nearby headstone washed by a storm
to the ground; the shovel blade holds
it all—the tears and the grass and the rain's
borrowed scent covers the dead
with a choir of things to hold. Song
in the mother mourning, mourning
what is left to hold, holding her one
long note, holding on to its impossible

fermata, to the throat's quaking acreage,
to the diaphragm's bellow; the note holds on
and won't let go, is shaped by this holding,
and is changed by the woman it enters
and changes. Song is changed. She is changed.
And the city is lightless, O God so still.

I called his name but heard my own
come back. In the fog of my breath
a prayer like wool too worn out to warm.
How long does it take a city to discover
how to separate the dead from the soon-dead?
I cut from grief a frieze. Depicted: blood river
let loose for the *why?* Who'd recognize me
without a head? Fear didn't have a face
to reveal. In the sinew, a raveling
truth: Osiris yet found—no one can teach how
the rest of us will speak without our mouths.

~

The rest of us will speak without our mouths.
Truth: Osiris yet found—no one can teach how
to reveal. In the sinew, a raveling
without a head. Fear didn't have a face
let loose for the *why?* Who'd recognize me?
I cut from grief a frieze. Depicted: blood river,
how to separate the dead from the soon-dead.
How long does it take a city to discover
a prayer like wool too worn out to warm?
Come back. In the fog of my breath
I called his name but heard my own.

A friend tells me he was attacked with a half-
empty cup of cola and *faggot*, both thrown from
a passing car's window late in the evening.

How enter a body not mine and speak
with the cadence of an activist with cola splashing
across sneakers? Narrative tries on its beauty,
its already-passed threshold into darker possibilities.

A boy's single district has become many
and every violence echoes Rashawn, echoes silence.

My friend, that it could happen again comforts (you live)
and frightens (could die). Again returning
to unseen tortures to enliven them. A newspaper
blows from my hands to the ground. Will I, too,
forget my dead brother and turn my head like a page?

as though to repair as though breakage as though
    bone-absence required could be sutured by silver
        glints brass and wrist turn a name unpuzzled

mind unpuzzles old technology flesh made artifact
    unabbreviated though this evidence unevidenced found
        distraction thrown out of the case of tools

as though a body gives its weight to sorrow so all
    is needed for all the sorrow is it
        so bad to sew shut a case with a clue

to borrow a screw here a plier there a bolt a case
    needs answers needs to look deeper inside
        a ruin no one can hold all of needs to

force light into where light cannot be missing

"[...] DNA evidence proved that an empty black bag sitting in the subway tunnel was used to carry the victim's corpse"—NYDailyNews.com (8-29-2008)

Witness: The Duffel Bag recalls dismemberment

Where was I?

Once to the subway, twice to the recycling plant,
I was carried then emptied of my gift. Each time
was like a dream I'd had: power tools rusting
against my zipper mouth, fingerprints stained
against a hammer's handle, expansion,
retraction—metallic lung, inchoate darkness.

Ice crammed in cups of folded feet
stole the final warmth, his hands
stretched across snow-spun air,
his body odor becoming mine.
Already his heart as though my own;
his hands fumbled his loosened seams.

Once to the subway, I was left near a trash bag by my carrier. When he held me, we didn't speak to one another. I don't know his story.

I was carried then emptied of everything I knew: hammer, flathead, monkey wrench, toenail clipper, Bible against the cross of a tire iron, a knife for each Commandment.

Was like a dream—my carrier's hands, leaning phone lines blown upright, stone pedestrian faces.

Against my zipper mouth dangles a miniature lock. With what would you test the dark belly of the fissure, unlock skin till it clicks and slides from itself a lit candle? Tell me, what would be the point, then, to see?

Against a hammer's handle. Against the cold likeness of a doorknob to both question and answer.

Retraction. Sometimes my carrier would reach inside for a blade but pull back, could not, for the life of him, make a choice.

Ice crammed in cups of water sounds like bones. No one listens. They are still alive not to.

Stole the final bit of warmth from the days that have passed, from my carrier, *his hands*

stretched across snow to feel some sensation. He stretches his collection before him in an arc across the ground, his breath a gray orb of *spun air.*

His body odor is ghost. You cannot arrest a killer you can't find. He is nothing and everything you are looking for. All of his secrets *becoming mine.*

Already his heart as though my own. There is a pulse in me and I call it nothing. I allow a breeze to slip past each zipper tooth. Please. I cannot speak. I hold it all in.

His hands fumble his loosened seams.
Already his heart as though my own,
becoming mine.
His body odor—as spun air—
stretched across snow
from his hands,
stole the final warmth—ice
crammed in cups, retracting
against a hammer's handle,
against my zipper mouth,
like a dream
I carried and emptied
once on the subway.

Dear Ms. Brazell-Jones,

        In an interview, I heard you say
a woman knocked on your door to condemn you
and Rashawn to hell, to preach
about gay sin after your son's death. Before
my grandfather died he said, *You cannot love a god
that you fear.* I want to but can't apologize
for the blade of that woman's faith, for every door
you enter but never exit.

Headline] "Gay Beau Sought in Body-Chop Slay" [Interrupted

Tell the story *another burst* of *difficult publicity   tragic in-the-making*
It's been eight years in the making   this *vigil* that has not ended

Tell how a city phantoms a boy   phantoms all witnesses
Anonymous woman called *during* America's Most Wanted *then hung up*

A woman who knew the unknown   *disappeared   blended into the crowd*
At a march for justice   the promise   *$22,000 reward if you have*

Helpful information   kept in the strictest of confidence that I don't have
Arrest the single photo of Brazell tuxedoed   *seeking information*

From a still frame   not *solving* the space between murder and *found*
Say *gregarious   life of the party   funny   studying Web design*   say people

Gravitated naturally to him   say he knew his killer   his killer knew him
He was my best friend his mother said   *leading* us into her memory

It's been ten *years*   and all that's recalled is *dismembered   1-800-577-*
TIPS   with my tongue's tip I might be *helpful*   this small noise I give

Witness reminisces while chewing gum

There were two pairs of feet twin-tapping: :Each as rhythmic as the other: :Waiting's rhythm not for train but a moment: :Like when the flavor's gone all gone and you saved the aluminum wrapper to spit: :I heard next impatience becoming: :Tapping out faster: :Nerves: :Train came but no one exited and the whole time tap tap tap each swifter than the last: :Sudden stop: :Weight: :Gravity wanted inside of me: :What does it mean to be like sound: :How does a body become sound: :I say now to listen: :Even now I sing inhale exhale: :You know: :Even now I'm rocking back and forth in my seat swallowing hard: :I saw closeness: :A familiarity between them easy to mistake as dangerous: :Duffel bag carried by the one looking back: :I turned my head away then back and both were gone: :Now this newspaper puts a dead boy where I was: :My past seeing: :Is it them the headline tells me I saw: :This face a dead boy's but I only remember the train's face erasing the track beneath it: :Lights thrown across the tunnel wall: :Red then red then gone

Searching for Rashawn Brazell (search performed 3-14-13)

1.   www.RashawnBrazell.com

"This page is in Japanese. Would you like to translate it?"

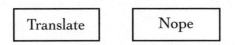

Selected translation: hand jobs learn how to you alone in the office the only man not so much with a woman purchase please with your credit card sex-shop life to health

2.   www.RashawnBrazell.com/index.html

        Not Found

Dear Ms. Brazell-Jones,

      I love my brother who wasn't a brother of mine.
Walking in an alley alone at night I bury my hands
in my pockets to appear brotherless, bordered
by the decay blowing from the stench.
To appear brotherless is to appear beyond help,
though you quoted Rashawn saying, *No one
is beyond help.* Some believe only the already-
destroyed are safe. I try to appear broken in order
to appear unbreakable, not worth further breaking.

Brooklyn lost a boy in the subway.
come back. In the fog of my breath
Of course the sky unbraids itself,
How long does it take a city to discover
Grief is a knife. Someone knew how
I cut a frieze. Depicted: blood river,
All limbs are undressed by the blade.
without a head? Fear didn't have a face,
didn't lead back to the butcher. Cleave
truth. Orpheus, Osiris — teach how.
to run, leave the rest behind.

I called his name but heard my own
called his name and a train replied,
a prayer like wool too worn out to warm.
a cloudscreen stitch quivers, a mirage?
to separate the dead from the soon-dead.
how to perform peculiar incisions.
Who'd recognize me
red-wet, separated. Cartographic meat
to reveal in the sinew a raveled direction,
Ask knee how to bend,
The rest of us will speak without our mouths.

This lightless city, this steel
god gone off to sleep
in the restless blood
bone-absence required. What is
the space between apology
and warning? I called his name
but heard *Let's go* fill
the air. I hold it all
in this restless mouth—
red, red—this small noise
I give. This imagined honor.
Me a small noise, me without
a mouth. This throat scorched
by the truth—say it—not found.

III

Door to a War I Never Knew

Javelin honeyed in a gladiator's blood, smoke masking
the sun with its cloak of slow owls, nurse praying over
a man whose ears and tongue have met blade—leave me.
My mind has little desire for you, you, and you, yet you all
insist like fog, like a complaint you stay. So stay and leave
the leaving to me, past this place with weather the smell
of iron, the sky heavy as weapons I've never held.

~

The farthest sight is the serrated underbite of cityscape
erect on the horizon, high rises pleated with suicides.
No one feels unsafe or loved in this fluorescence
of small privacies. Sky pocked with skiffs of gaslight,
what promises mount the work-hammered spines
beneath you? Here be fortunes and fortresses.
Who could turn their back to them and survive?

Love Story

I was told I could turn my back to them,
the sickle-mouthed angels who rummage
through the church dumpsters looking
for wings or food. One is a friend, febrile
with addiction, drug-rot blackened teeth
freaked into blades from the sheath of his lips.
I was told he would occupy no space
in my memory, that he shouldn't. Snow
falls like a mask in pieces over his face.

~

Rachel comes to the porch holding herself and asking for
my uncle. We say he gone to the store but he's years dead.
She keeps holding on to herself like her body remembers
what her mind lost. *When he get back, tell him he owe me $5.*
We offer to pay. She says, *No. Tell him.*

No, Tell Him—

—when winter makes his grave twice sepulchral,
that ice evanesces eventually back
to green, the closet of stuck time unsticking.

To see him means to see air without
him, seas of dust where his feet could interrupt,
a shipwreck no one knew to need.

~

Then it was spring. The alluvial earth of grief
found its hoof's bottom and went. Madly
pastoral, cornhusk-rigid and resolute,
morning stayed without pathos, stayed
the doom-frost heart till the hard of it splayed.

Then getting over it had to be redone. Daily,
a door to step through. Daily the hostile enigma:
to enter, turn the knob though the knob will burn.

LUMINOUS, WHATEVER HONEY

I go to twist the knob of a burning skull
that burns because the canyon sun has touched
curve after curve of the hard, soiled thing
into luminosity, as though veins ran courses
around the buffered ivory of socket and tooth,
rounded where thinking broke loose.
Coyote skull? Fox skull? I'm too ignorant
to know. The elaborate bone's circled by opulence:
cactus blossoms, a beetle's green carapace. My thumb
falls into where sight's gone hollow. My fingers
fondle the spinal gap for whatever sap's
left over in the desiccated jaw. Whatever honey
was eaten has calcified, as though hunger has frozen
under skin, over thought, in the tremble of my hand.

REND

Hands trembling, they wash their bodies
with lamplight to show what night
can call them to. Each other, mostly, drawing
shadows on the wall: shark tooth
divining the tide, an egg hiding the last shard
of moon inside albumen. The eagle
they make transforms into hydra, into
cypress dropping then bringing up again its leaves.

~

A story lives on in the mind: a contest,
the king and his servant combat, a need for both
to become the other, the crown never the object.
Their contortion a rose bruised on every petal, wrecked
out of itself for symbol, for its velvet deftly ground,
from which the shade of *resist, don't* can be found.

OF CONTOUR, OF CADENCE

Resist, don't: the difference between what one thinks
the magnolias say—branches applauding
some animal act below—and what
they actually say…nothing

                   between us can
we prepare for, only postpone. I've learned

to plead and to please, another difference.

         ~

Turn your face that way where light no more
transfigures you than darkness makes a need for
transfiguration. Yes, the scar above your eye.

Blood had dropped from the wound, a curtain.

But I believe we are, inside, all blue, you said.
Listen, neither we nor blue make sky.
The earth spins and we, utterly, are spun.

GREATLY BE GENTLE

In the night-spun clearing we were spent, star-burst wide
and lending our skin to the sun's failing heat.

Where your hand sat, my clavicle met, unbending.
Where are your arrows to pull this bow-bone taut
till timid, till cracked so night could crawl its way inside?

Was a sharpness where you weighted yourself against me.
Was a blind spot in my body's breakage, where tightness
Was soldiered away, spread well-winged and with blade.

~

A dream in my night broke my sleep.
I only remember waking to streetlights
through the window, a dull yellow
washing over everything. My darkness
a lighter shade of itself. On my bare chest,
light masked the door to the dream.

IV

OFTEN I AM PERMITTED TO RETURN TO THE CITY

as if it were a scene made up by my need
for a city, viaducts July-sweating sweat not

mine as the city is no longer mine, was never,
but it holds me near to its metallic, junkyard
pasture and junkie song so hollow it's a hall

I dare not walk through, this tragic place
wherefrom the people with my face fall.

Wherefrom fall all the architectures I am
I say are my people's people and my people
whose houses tremble as thunderous bass passes.

The blacktopped roads sop up heat for double
Dutch feet to greet, rope slapped down
by a child's hand. I used to know her name.

It is only a dream of trees, their propeller seeds
blown west through batches of weeds crocheted
yellow-green with dandelions and cigarette butts

once erect from a mouth stressed over rent due,
dried spit the tincture of wait and liquor stores.

Often I am permitted to return to this city
as if it were a gift for which I forgot the means
to augur into clarity, always wrapped in cool violence,

neighbors' frowns cauterized into cul-de-sacs,
omen outcasting what lives to give relief.

OF DARKER CEREMONIES

after E. 1999 Eternal *by Bone Thugs-N-Harmony*

Dear god of armed robberies and puff-puff-pass,
a chalk outline unpeels from the street, smashes
every windshield, and leaves florid temples of crack
on porches. Burnt-black pleats of joint-pressed lips
prophesied your return. Please accept these nickel bags
as offerings. Brick bastions of piss-stench thresholds
and boarded windows require a weekly sacrifice.
Is there a tarot card called "The Corner," a shrike
shown lifting a corpse from the pike of a middle finger?
Children speak to their murdered brothers with a cereal box
and construction paper cut into a Ouija's tongue that licks
yes when asked if liquor could polish a skull in a way
pleasing to the dead, licks *no* when asked for a name.

A SURVEY OF MASCULINITY

My horse, my stallion, I ride you unprivate
through whispery villages. Falter not
from their gossip that you were once a man
mimicking an animal's affectionless muscle
to become more man. Bury beneath
your hooves' hopscotch these upright beasts
caught in night's sleight of hand branding *omen*
in their hair and meat. Watch boys be forced
into men by men who've forgotten their own
forcing. Haloes of flies bite the boymen as mules
slobber through wheezy chaff and bridle in a district
of hands. Gaze of denotation, of well-bred
taxidermy, of ghouls misnamed Mandingo
till the weight of their manhood stuck
like a mannerism. Is it loving men that removes
my manacled mouth, mutes my mule dick's howl
as the gelding knife lands? In this land manicured
by manure and blood, hyacinth and bullets, the tool
and the temper rule while the suicides of sons
feed the softened earth beneath our stampede.
I, too, could learn to neigh and drop dead in this
claustrophobic strobe of fireflies at my flank.
Some beasts were trained to eat their own. Some
were trained to flinch at their own reflections.

APOTHEOSIS

We are back to the beginning and have gone
inside. The bats have come down, wooden

and sterile, to greet the joints, to rearrange
teeth and thoughts. Faggot was a thought

that snuck inside me, was put inside me,
and all the fields inside me turned Greek,

meaning tragic, meaning its beasts
were hybrid and hard to slay:

a faggot in the nigger, a nigger and a faggot
and though both hollered I couldn't let them go.

~

Still this is a faggot's tale, and he says: *tired*
of the new prescriptions of the world, I woke

to the bass of a stranger's Hummer but thought
I remained, still, in my violent dream. He said,

Maybe
there isn't a thing to keep this blood from draining.

Yet having felt the heat in me shake like a window,
this moment's an unhinging, a loosened fiber ("pussy

nigga" from the Hummer, "batty bwoy" in the dream)
taking possession of this thinking. So the faggot man said.

It was how the word made dark his every room: faggot
the only definition for faggot, a measured burn

at the edge of sleep. To see in his dream a fire
ant crawl from the eye of a dead crow, to see himself

as the dead crow and not the ant, to know he was
the crow in sleep and when awake—it was the sharp

of the word that sharpened itself, teaching him
how to describe himself, faggot like a new lexicon,

and it entered him, became a childhood
memory: faggot in a house in a cradle full of sticks lit

at their tips like cigarillos: faggot tied to the wheel
of his family's iris and spun and cudgeled: *Faggot where*

you going this late at night: faggot where a pit bull
pirouettes another pit bull in its mouth: faggot who faggots

flagrantly his gilded gums with hurrah and haints:
faggot in the fly horde sucking at a corpse-supple wound

stitch by stitch until the fabric pops open:
fabric pops open and the wind moves through: faggot

coming in like the wind: how the wind comes again
when it can but different than it had been: a storm

that was both weapon and shield until already
it had entered where neither — anymore — mattered.

Do-rag

O darling, the moon did not disrobe you.
You fell asleep that way, nude
and capsized by our wine, our bump

n' grind shenanigans. Blame it
on whatever you like; my bed welcomes
whomever you decide to be: hung-

mistress, bride's bouquet, John Doe
in the alcove of my dreams. You
can quote verbatim an entire album

of Bone Thugs-N-Harmony with your ass
in the air. There's nothing
wrong with that. They mince syllables

as you call me yours. You don't
like me but still invite me to your home
when your homies aren't near

enough to hear us crash into each other
like hours. Some men have killed
their lovers because they loved them

so much in secret that the secret kept
coming out: wife gouging her husband
with suspicion, churches sneering

when an usher enters. Never mind that.
The sickle moon turns the sky into
a man's mouth slapped sideways

to keep him from spilling what no one would
understand: you call me god when it
gets good though I do not exist to you

outside this room. Be yourself or no one else
here. Your do-rag is camouflage-patterned
and stuffed into my mouth.

HE LOVED HIM MADLY

[In a Silent Way]
It had been watching you sleep in dreams of excrement
and hard voices. The government gifted it with mute,
unregulated hands. It came to you, father, before
I was born, my bones bound in the cup of your absence.
Your skin was peeled in a dominion of wolves.

[Illegal Business]
When it came it came wearing familial faces.
House after house, noses took in this new air.
A brother OD'd, a father, a mother, an uncle, a sister —
House after house cataracted with snow-veiled skulls.
On the corner, police officers licked their white fingers.

[Will O' the Wisp]
I was four when I committed your face
to memory. I made into reason what was
once rumor. Diaspora, meaning this time
what father-source had left me pliant had
returned so that I could return and turn to it.

[Dead Presidents II]
Poverty gave reason to hustle. A dealer's
frozen wrists, weighted by stones, flipped
through green pages of an anemic bible
that cataloged white men who once jeweled their own
properties in varicose coffles toward cotton coffins.

[Black Comedy]
Father, you were summarized by your veins' laughter.
Last time I saw you your face was cratered
with breathless mouths collaborating with dust.
Behold the white horse, hoof over hoof
dispersing the circus of our communal horror.

[Ten Crack Commandments]
It's offensive, our most brilliant forced to pray
to getting paid, forced to spray or get sprayed.
It got so bad folks was scraping and sniffing
the ash off their knees. Cities full of prophets
that could only see as far as their own decease.

[Inamorata]
Whom did you love most: Lady Caine, Mama Coca,
White Lady, Girlfriend, Lady Snow, Pearl,
Aunt Nora, Angie, Carrie Nation, Percia, Mujer,
Corrinne, Gift-of-the-Sun-God, Snow White, Her?

[Dope]
Cain't be capitalism. No suh! No suh! u u u u u u u
Must be the Devil! Cain't be white supremacy! No suh!
Couldn'ta been the Iran-ContraaffairandReaganlooking
underTOWmissilesforhostageswhileCIAbreaksloaves
ofcokealloverthisGodfearinland no suh! u u u u u owowoo!

[Sorcerer]
Father, I have sewn my eyes to an allegiance
with worms. I am still incredulous of light.
The city of my teeth has softened its curses.
If you arrived elemental, shapeless and aquiver,
I'd fashion you a suit from my hollow's frame.

67

[C.R.E.A.M]
How much for the faux Bearden of a Lexus collaged
over a crack house, addicts clawing the air like trees?
When weight moves like poltergeists a triple beam
gets its wings, but not all caine is able.

[On the Corner]
The moon unbraids a man's hair. His Solo Cup
of Jack Daniels catches light, shakes to the bass
rattle of speakers stacked on the porch like die.
His woman leans on his shoulder. When he kisses
her forehead he leaves a bouquet of stars.

[Street Dreams]
Her blunt unrolled itself on the floor. Its entrails rose
and configured like a burning church in reverse.
Then her grandpa's voice: *Baby, this ain't no place
of worship*. But she already had a messenger, had
already counted the buds blooming from her tongue.

[Recollections]
My father sang in Superior Movement. He would croon
around the house, the halls carrying his falsetto
like a good beast. In the store he gave me quarter
after quarter to play *Pac-Man* and *Golden Axe*.
He taught me to laugh at losing, how to run away fast.

[Let Me Roll]
Lung rider, smoke inscriber, your eyes spin white,
coaxed inward by black steers stomping loose
their hair to string your mind's cavity into heirloom
and guitar. To you the air is erotic, is panic-stricken.
Your bloodshot eyes weave a nest to nest the haints.

[He Loved Him Madly]
Dear architect of rot. Dear razor that is your dead body
beneath my bare feet. Dear smile, endless, a lake
that keeps my reflection. Dear reflection I keep
in the locket of my closed eyes. Dear father.
Dear wish. Dear closest thing to God I know.

ELEGGUA AND ESHU AIN'T THE SAME

I'm listening to Alice Coltrane to feel Blacker than God
while I pull gray hairs out my head. One wish, two wish.
I can't stand my own body. My body can't stand itself
so my head hair spirals like rivers storming up
to the sky. My hands are ashy and Jergens don't help,
might as well use water. Might as well turn my fingers
into the rivers my sister's ex-boyfriend taught me.
The strange ways men touch each other, the codices
writing themselves in tribes. *Don't forget. You can't forget.*
What colors could I wear more dangerous
than the one I was born with, collard greens
and cigarette smoke in my clothes, Johnny Walker
strutting down my uncles' throats. When one wilds out
his brother rubs his back. *You a damn fool.* Some blues
got in the potato salad. Some "Wang Dang Doodle"
found a home in my ten-year-old hips. My body don't
give a damn about me like my mind do. Growing up,
I snapped Barbie's head from her body. I snapped
like Chaka Khan at the end of "Through the Fire."
There is rage in the chicken fried so hard
the bones edible. I suck on the marrow to blacken
my gums. Somebody pulled out the Crown Royal
bag to find a quarter and a shirt button, sewed
that shit in on the spot and gave a neighbor bus fare.
"I'm Going Down" is playing and I can't tell which
woman is singing it. Must be Rose Royce cause her sorrow
don't sound like Mary's dirge though they both got two
sets of wings sprouting from their lips. *All God's Chillun Got…*

and someone reneges at the table and we all ignore
the gunshots down the street. Our names not on
the bullets. They aim around here. Spade cut a heart
now a heart's on the table breaking hearts. When am I?
I'm sixteen and watching a friend rub the blue dye
off a boy's jeans onto her white pants, ass looking
like a spring sky. His face humiliated with lust.
Was it Aaliyah or Outkast that got her jinxing color
from cloth, coaxing a boy into manhood that faded
swiftly? *Me and you…your mama and your cou-sin too*,
sneaking us liquor on the back porch, birthday cake
and shit talk in the air, somebody back inside
raging about high school beef. Kick his ass
out the party. Let him stand by the door, be security.
Can't let everybody in the house. I'm back
with my family and my sister's playing with the dead
again, crying to the glossolalia of "Tha Crossroads."
The one white boy we had on the block got shot.
They called him Cornflake. I don't know
what year I'm in anymore. Eazy-E dead,
Tupac and Biggie still breathing. The Isley Brothers
sing "Make Me Say It Again Girl" and my sis and I sing
what we know: *Make me say—so you won't be lonely*.
The generations have conspired against me.
River in my head. I'm pulling and pulling. Somebody
in my head want out. I stopped singing in church
when the songs didn't make the dead come back.
My rage stopped working, too. The cursing in shadows,
the shadow boxing. The house so safe it wasn't
safe no more. I must've hid that part of me under
the doorstep outside. Went back to look and I was gone.

VISITATION

—or it was night that entered, tar-hued
and moved inside me new blood. Its star-
pocked fists gave the promise of bats.
I waited for their leather to spill into my window,
for their tiny throats to blow and trill. A bell
some miles away—bats in its mouth—loved
the taste and swayed. Here is a hunger to stir
me. A man could live in the blur
of a hundred hearts, could learn to tame
the eager clapper, which is loneliness
testing the marrow and waking what's within:
scatter-song, blind and coming on like skin.

FOR JOY BE RIGHTEOUS

"I wonder who will sing for me when I am gone"

No one crawl-voiced enough, no one shawl-
throated and tall tale torqueing sleep into night-
mare can neigh like the hinges of your casket-
taut joints, can sing brighter than the birds of church
hats when fans lift frills that veil a brown seeing.

In what torment and why do you find that song
is necessary adieu? *Farewell,* not in the dirt
landing over your body, not in the burgundy
crease the departing sun leaves behind. Farewell
discourteous dead-not-yet. My friend, won't tears

be enough? Won't the hollow piped wings
tearing from behind you sting enough to amnesia
you from recognizing any longer a human voice?
The small animal in you thrusts for sky, rises out.

SELVAGE

A Rottweiler is the shadow of an angel of vengeance.
The dog blows out a star's light while scratching
its ribs. It augers the fallen leaves like tarot, decodes
the hot scales of a salamander as it burns through
a cave's void. It watches the just-born children
like watching a dream it cannot wake from. When it claws
its own grave in a junkyard to the voice of Bessie Smith
tumbling from a transistor radio, it stays for good.

There is a pack of them, ravaged, made savage
by cage and raw meat, BB gun pellets shot
into their faces till the red ponds of their wounds
spill down. The cold ovals of metal chain interlock
jowls against the onyx fur of dogs stolen
from their owners. Howls scar the night. Some beasts
bite when fear tells them to. They destroy other dogs
and the angel of their shadows looks away.

In their old age, where do fighting dogs go? Where
rest their abused bodies made four-legged hauntings?
These precise lovers forced into vicious servitude,
their eyes rejecting moonlight, shake at first when held,
having not known such softness. Bathed and brushed
they whimper, are hushed. Softly, they begin to snore.

EPITHALAMIUM

A kiss. Train ride home from a late dinner,
City Hall and document signing. Wasn't cold
but we cuddled in an empty car, legal.
Last month a couple of guys left a gay bar
and were beaten with poles on the way
to their car. No one called them faggot
so no hate crime's documented. A beat down
is what some pray for, a pulse left to count.
We knew we weren't protected. We knew
our rings were party favors, gold to steal
the shine from. We couldn't protect us,
knew the law wouldn't know how. Still, his
beard across my brow, the burn of his cologne.
When the train stopped, the people came on.

OF SHADOWS AND MIRRORS

A ghost floats between my father's ghost
and me. Haunt me if you want, history,
bough's shadow looming through
my window and across my neck
where an umbilical cord had once claimed
each yet-born breath. When I die I'll die
clutching final words on the final inhale. I think
if I don't speak then maybe I won't die.
I remember the last time I saw my father yellowed
and bejeweled with drug-rot and face craters
where skin tried to hide in skin. Even today,
the base of my family tree fumes alcohol
and smoke from still-hot circles
of crack pipes. My mother's Caesarian
means she birthed me as tragedy hidden in bloody regalia,
royalty scared of choking on bark broken
from the husk of an addicted man. I love him
despite his struggle for home-coming, to have
a throne and not a grave that looks like lips
folding in when rain weakens the muddy perimeter.
The darkness to fear is not the darkness
earth makes of itself but what earth would tell us
if it parted those lips, emptied its sweet
sweet house. My grandfather salted every threshold
to keep evil from entering his house. I heard
that salt stinging an open wound means its cleaning
out demons, but maybe its crystal mirrors

are unwelcome, the body never wanting to see
its own inner ugly. Would that we could
make any pair of eyes see us new. Musicians
play for survival on every other corner
in the Delmar Loop. One man leans deep into
the chords, into the hollow where nylon stretches
to capture his sweat's salt so nothing darker
than the pit of the guitar can get inside or get out.
In the pit of addiction my father was almost run down
by my mother on the south side of Chicago, genetic
near-blindness had him walking in the streets
with only his ears and feet to tell if a bus
would greet him before a Chevy's grill. Was in
a bevy of reeds by a filthy lake on the west side
where I heard a whistle break from the stalks
and imagined a bodiless head calling for its body.
Why leave behind a head unless it's always led to danger
or boredom, the advent of dark flirtation?
What else did my father hear in a speeding car's
screech and horn? My mother barely recognized
the torn down man and he didn't see her at all,
squinting between high and death. It's death
that blinds with excess clarity, like seeing someone
stripped to his essentials, a tree minus nest or leaf.
Unburied bones critique the dusk, sharp as a branch
on a signless road. Where turn for the next
hunger? How long until these small mouths fill?

BIRTH OF THE DOPPELGÄNGER

A wolf's entrails opened and I stepped
into them. I stepped into the jowls

of the dead, into the stench. Flies scoured
the decayed innards like priests washing temple walls.

It was ecstatic, the flipped-over car,
wolf teeth shining from gum swell above

tongue, behind cheek, after blood spill
and my car spilled until all hell spilled and you

want to know what the taste was like?
I tell you at the crash's wake

was a new life. My new self
bled out from the old self. I left

behind a husk pricked by daggers
of wood and lungs drunk off exhaust.

Saw the one eye left in the split skull watch
my skin roll up like panty hose over the bones,

over pristine muscle blood hot and fresh.
I walked away from car and corpse and made

room for nothing but this body's
first words. See my mouth move, like this—

notes

"Inheritance: The Force of Aperture" considers the murder of Eric Glover and Terrence Rankins in Joliet, IL. by the hands of four individuals who strangled the two and attempted to dismember them. It was later discovered that two of the suspects (possibly three) had sex on their corpses. All four of the suspects were white, while both of the victims were black, spurring a debate as to whether this could be considered a hate crime. The poem also considers the lynching of three black circus workers—Elias Clayton, Elmer Jackson, and Isaac McGhie—in Duluth, MN, after a mob of 5,000 dragged the alleged rapists from their jail cells, harming themselves and police officers during the process. In the image, two men are hanged on a post while the other man is left dead on the ground. The postcard is marked Oct, 1919 when in fact the lynching took place June 15, 1920. For further information, please refer to *Without Sanctuary* by James Allen.

"Inheritance: Anthem":
The second section is for Lamar. The third section quotes Beyoncé, "I woke up like dis," from her track "Flawless" and quotes Talib Kweli, "But I never write to remain silent," from his track "Stand to the Side."

"Witness":
Rashawn Brazell had plans to go to college. Inspired by his mother, Desire Brazell-Jones, he wanted to work with communities in need. He was interested in web design and designing his own wardrobe. He deconstructed other items of clothing to make his own clothes. He visited the community center The Door and volunteered his time as a mentor and tutor for younger children. For more information, visit the podcast OPEN YOUR MIND with Terik King, season 2, episode 5—"The Rashawn Brazell Case," published 1-26-2010, where much of this information was found.

Italicized words come from "Gay Beau Sought in Body-Chop Slay" by Larry Celona, *NY Post* (3-20-2006); "Unsolved butchering of 19-year-old Rashawn Brazell enters eighth year without any leads after his body was found in dark Brooklyn subway tunnel" by Pete Donohue, *New York Daily News* (2-24-2013); and a bulletin requesting information about Rashawn Brazell's murder issued by the Anti-Violence Project and People of Color in Crisis.

The section, "Witness: The duffle bag recalls dismemberment" takes its form from Mary Cornish's poem "Fifteen Moving Parts" from her book *Red Studio*.

The partial quote from Ms. Brazell-Jones, "…and I want the rest of my child," is from a *The New York Times* article "A Year After a Teenager Was Dismembered, Still No Answer" (Feb. 13, 2006).

"Often I am Permitted to Return to the City" takes its title and structure from Robert Duncan's poem "Often I am Permitted to Return to a Meadow."

"A Survey of Masculinity" is after Aime Césaire's poem "Horse."

"Apotheosis" is after "Cross Country" by Roger Reeves.

"He Loved Him Madly" is a partial (15-section) pecha kucha for my father, Calvin Ford, and uses titles from Miles Davis compositions (odd-number stanzas) and various Hip Hop and spoken word tracks (even-number stanzas). In order of appearance, artists of the even-number stanzas are Boogie Down Productions, Jay-Z, The Notorious B.I.G., Amiri Baraka, Wu-Tang Clan, Scarface, and Nas.

"For Joy Be Righteous" takes its epigraph from Roger Reeves.

BOOK BENEFACTORS

Alice James Books wishes to thank the following individuals who generously contributed toward the publication of *Thief in the Interior:*

Benjamin Goldberg
Evan Kleekamp
Matthew Nienow

For more information about AJB's book benefactor program, contact us via phone or email, or visit alicejamesbooks.org to see a list of forthcoming titles.

Recent Titles from Alice James Books

Alice James Books has been publishing poetry since 1973. The press was founded in Boston, Massachusetts as a cooperative wherein authors performed the day-to-day undertakings of the press. This collaborative element remains viable even today, as authors who publish with the press are also invited to become members of the editorial board and participate in editorial decisions at the press. The editorial board selects manuscripts for publication via the press's annual, national competition, the Alice James Award. Alice James Books seeks to support women writers and was named for Alice James, sister to William and Henry, whose extraordinary gift for writing went unrecognized during her lifetime.

Designed by Pamela A. Consolazio
LITTLE FROG DESIGNS

Printed by McNaughton & Gunn